Know your Pet

QEB

DOGS and Puppies

Michaela Miller

QEB Publishing

QEB

First published in the United States in 2006 by
QEB Publishing, Inc.
23062 La Cadena Drive
Laguna Hills, CA 92653
www.qeb-publishing.com

Library of Congress Control Number: 2005911052

ISBN 978-1-59566-218-7

Written by Michaela Miller
Consultant Chris Laurence QVRM, TD, BCSc, MRCVS, Veterinary Director at Dogs Trust
Designed by Melissa Alaverdy
Editor Louisa Somerville
Pictures supplied by Warren Photographic

Publisher Steve Evans
Editorial Director Jean Coppendale
Art Director Zeta Davies

Printed and bound in China

Words in **bold** are explained in the glossary on page 30.

Contents

The right dog for you

Dogs make wonderful pets. They love to play, walk, and run with their owners and be part of the family. But dogs can also be hard work, so think carefully about what's involved before you decide to give a dog or puppy a home.

It's your choice! Labrador puppies come in three colors: chocolate, yellow, and black.

Is a dog for me?

To find out if a dog is the right pet for you and your family, here are some questions to ask each other:

🐾 Will we be happy to take care of a dog, even when it is sick or old?

🐾 Will we take it for walks twice a day, even if it is wet and cold outside?

🐾 Will we make sure that the dog is never left on its own for more than three hours during the day?

🐾 Do we have an escape-proof yard so the dog can play outside safely?

🐾 Can we afford to pay the vet for our dog's yearly vaccinations and for any other care it might need?

🐾 When we go on vacation, can we afford to keep our dog in a kennel, if we can't take it with us?

If you can answer "yes" to all the questions, a dog could be the pet for you!

4

Dogs, dogs, dogs

Dogs come in all shapes and sizes, from tiny Chihuahuas to huge Great Danes. They also have different **temperaments**, so try to choose one that suits your family. For example, a large boisterous dog such as a flat-coated retriever or Border collie might not be good with small children, who could get hurt if knocked down. A smaller dog with a calm and friendly temperament might be better. As well as purebred dogs (see page 9) such as Labradors and spaniels, there are lots of mixed-breed dogs—or mutts —that make great pets.

Big or small, long or short—haired, there are so many types of dogs!

Dog or puppy?

Puppies are very appealing, but they need a lot of care. They need toilet training and obedience training and can also be messy and destructive. Adopting a full-grown dog from an animal shelter might be a better choice. Although adult dogs might take time to settle into a new home, they can make excellent pets. Before making a decision, why not get some advice from a vet?

On the wild side

All dogs are descended from wolves. People began keeping wolves as pets about 10,000–15,000 years ago, to protect their homes and herd their animals. Although this was long ago, learning about wolf behavior is helpful to understand how your own pet dog thinks. It can also help you to care for your dog the right way.

Different characteristics

After the first wolves were taken in and cared for, people started breeding them to have different **characteristics**. Dogs such as collies and sheepdogs were bred to herd farm animals. Some dogs, such as golden retrievers, were bred to find and retrieve (fetch) birds, or other animals the owner had hunted. Others, such as small poodles and Chihuahuas, were bred simply for companionship.

Wolves normally walk about 30 miles (50 km) a day in search of food. Your dog won't need to do that, but its instinct is still to keep busy. This is why regular walks and mental activity help keep your dog happy and healthy.

Wolves howl when they are separated from other pack members and to warn wolves from different packs to keep away. They may also howl when they have hunted down their prey.

Part of the pack

Wolves are social animals—they live in groups, known as packs. Like a wolf, your dog is a social animal and it needs a pack to make it happy. Your family is your new dog's pack! The dog needs to learn to have good relationships with the other members in the pack family, including accepting that it must do what it's told. If your dog doesn't learn how to behave when it's a puppy, then behavioral problems such as jumping up, growling when it shouldn't, biting, and aggression can develop.

Border collies are bred to work herding livestock, but in the right hands they can make wonderful pets.

How do dogs communicate?

Dogs have their own body language. An aggressive dog stands with its ears pricked up and head held high. It will stare, bare its teeth, and make the fur along its back stand up to make itself look bigger. It will also growl or bark and hold its tail straight out. If a dog is afraid, it might **cower** with its ears flattened and its teeth bared. It might whine and whimper. A friendly dog has its eyes wide open and its mouth looking as if it's smiling. Happy dogs often whimper or yap.

7

Choosing your puppy or dog

Do you want a pure breed or a mutt? If you want a purebred dog, you'll need to find a specialist who breeds and sells them. Training a puppy takes effort, so you might prefer to get an adult dog. Look in animal shelters, although a dog from a shelter may not be trained the way you want and you might need to spend time retraining it.

Purebreds

The American Kennel Club, which represents breeders from all over the country, is a good place to search for a purebred. Most breed clubs have websites that will help you find breeders in your area. There are also websites for organizations that specialize in looking after purebred dogs. Don't buy puppies through advertisements offering lots of different breeds. These may be dogs from puppy farms which do not care for their animals responsibly.

An eight-week-old German shepherd puppy enjoying a game.

Good puppy practice

Before you buy, make sure you see your puppy with its mother to get a good idea of the size of dog the puppy is likely to become. If its mother seems happy with people, then your puppy will probably be the same—if you bring it up right. Choose a puppy with a clean nose and teeth. It should have no signs of diarrhea around its tail and should walk without limping. If you are buying from a breeder, the puppy may have had its first vaccinations, and you should be given a diet sheet so you can give your dog the right food.

Pet stores sometimes sell puppies, but it's not a good idea to buy from them. Puppies from different litters are often kept together. Mixing puppies in this way, before they have had their vaccinations, means there is a high risk of disease spreading and of your puppy becoming sick.

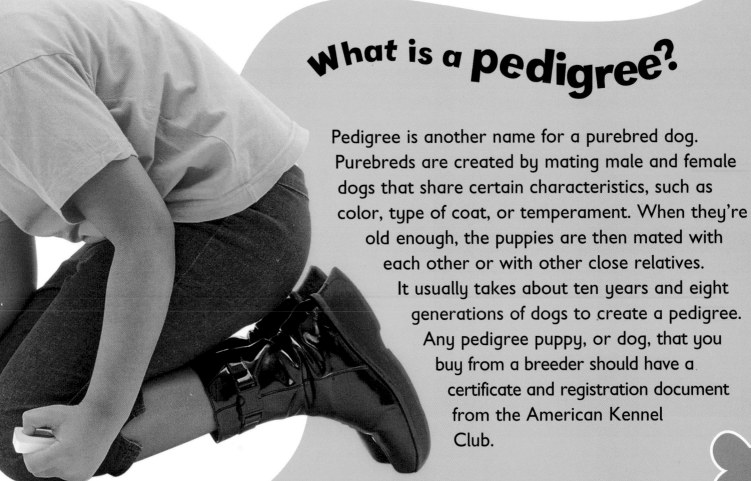

What is a pedigree?

Pedigree is another name for a purebred dog. Purebreds are created by mating male and female dogs that share certain characteristics, such as color, type of coat, or temperament. When they're old enough, the puppies are then mated with each other or with other close relatives. It usually takes about ten years and eight generations of dogs to create a pedigree. Any pedigree puppy, or dog, that you buy from a breeder should have a certificate and registration document from the American Kennel Club.

Adopting a dog from a shelter

Animal shelters are good places to look for dogs and puppies. If you and your family are thinking of adopting a homeless dog or puppy, ask your vet to recommend some local shelters.

Dogs from animal shelters can make excellent pets, but make sure that you choose one that will suit your family.

Asking questions

Good shelters will ask you questions to make sure that the dog is going to the right home. Most shelters also do home checks to make sure that you and your house and yard are right for a dog. You should also ask about the dog you'd like to adopt. The more you learn about it, the better. It would be heartbreaking to take a dog back to a shelter because you find that it can't get along with your cat, doesn't like children, or is scared of cars.

Pet payment

Most animal shelters expect you to make a donation or payment for the dog you take away, to show that you have made a commitment to your new pet. This money usually goes toward paying for some of the care it will have received at the shelter.

Most dogs and puppies that end up in animal shelters have been taken there, or abandoned, because their owners found that they could not care for a dog.

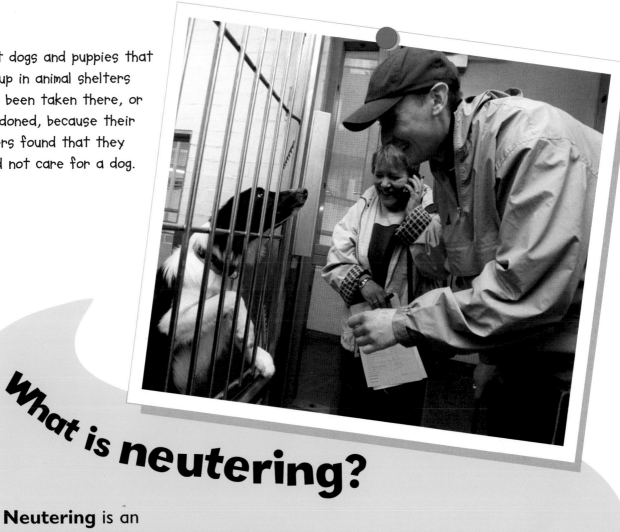

What is neutering?

Neutering is an operation that stops male dogs from being able to produce puppies. There are so many unwanted dogs that it's a good idea to get yours neutered. Neutering can help to prevent some types of cancer and other diseases as the dog grows older. Vets will advise you on the best time to have the operation. Dogs from shelters are usually neutered before you take them or, if you're adopting a puppy, you may have to take it back to be neutered when it's old enough.

Before you bring your new puppy or dog home, check whether you need a dog license in your state or county. Then make sure you have the right food and equipment ready.

Feeding time

The breeder or animal shelter should tell you what food your dog is used to, so make any changes gradually. Dogs of different sizes and ages need different amounts and types of food. A three-month-old puppy, for example, will need four meals a day of special puppy food. An adult dog may need feeding just once a day. Your dog must always have fresh water available, and its food bowl should be washed out daily.

Collars and leashes

Without a collar and leash, it is hard to train a dog to walk safely and to behave well. Your puppy will need a soft collar that's loose enough that you can fit two fingers between it and the puppy's neck. You'll also need a leash that clips on and off easily.

Check with the breeder or animal shelter about the right style of leash and collar for your type of dog.

Bedtime

Your dog's bed should be a non-chewable, rigid plastic basket that can be easily cleaned. Any bedding should be washable, too. The bed should be in a quiet place and never in an area that can get too hot, such as a sun room. Some owners put their puppy's bed inside a big cage or crate. The puppy learns to treat the crate as its den. Once it's used to it, your dog can be left inside its crate with the door shut for short times in the day when necessary. Crates can be a safe way to transport dogs in cars, too.

Make sure that your dog's basket is not in a drafty place.

Car travel

When you bring your puppy home, and for its first trips to the vet, it should travel in its crate or in a well-ventilated pet carrier. A dog can travel on the back seat of a car if wearing a harness attached to the seatbelt, and also in the rear compartment of a station wagon if secured safely. Never leave your dog in a car on a hot day, even in the shade with a window open. Temperatures in cars rise fast, and your dog could die in just a few minutes.

The first few days

The first few days in a new home can be quite a stressful time for a puppy. It will miss its mother and its brothers and sisters, and it will have lots of new things to get used to.

Gently does it

When you bring your puppy home, first take it into your yard so that it can go to the bathroom if it needs to. Then take it to the room that contains its bed, food, and water. Sit quietly and let it sniff around the room. Your puppy will come to you when it is ready. Make sure it goes outside after eating or drinking to go to the bathroom. Don't let your puppy go beyond the yard until it has had all of its vaccinations, as it could catch a disease.

Crate training

To introduce your puppy to its crate, make sure its bed, water, and a toy are already inside. The adult in charge of training should say "Into your crate!" in a cheerful voice and give the puppy a treat when it goes in. Leave the door open so it can leave at any time. Soon the puppy will happily go in and out of the crate and treat the crate as its special place. You can then close the door for a few minutes at a time.

Toilet training

To help puppies go to the bathroom in the right place, always take them outside when they wake up, after they have been playing, and after eating and drinking. Give them lots of praise when they go. A three-month-old puppy will usually need to go to the bathroom every three hours. Puppies should never be shouted at if they accidentally go to the bathroom indoors. This will only make them nervous. Simply say "No!" firmly and move them to their outdoor spot.

As your puppy gets used to its new home and owners, it will relax and become more confident.

Meeting other dogs and cats

If you have a crate, leave your puppy inside for short periods and give any other dogs or cats you have a chance to get used to its look and smell. When you let the puppy out, don't leave it alone with other pets until they are comfortable with each other. Be particularly careful introducing an adult dog to other household pets. Keep it on its leash. It can take several weeks for animals to get used to each other. Don't leave them alone together during this time.

Grooming and handling

Grooming gets rid of dirt, loose hair, and dead skin and helps keep a dog's skin in good condition. It also strengthens the bond between you and your dog. While grooming, you can check for fleas and make sure that your dog's eyes and ears are clear of infections.

Brush work

For long-haired dogs, you will need a soft brush and a bristle brush, wide- and fine-toothed combs, and a stripping comb. Groom a short-haired dog with a rough mitt. Brush gently along its back and sides in the direction that your dog's fur grows, then underneath its tummy and around its tail. Comb long-haired areas and tangles very gently. Older dogs sometimes need to be washed with dog shampoo (but bathing too often can be bad for their coat).

If you aren't sure which brush is right for your dog, ask your vet.

Different types of dogs have different coats, and some will need more grooming than others. Long-haired dogs such as Afghan hounds, Yorkshire terriers, and golden retrievers need daily grooming.

Handling tips

Pet your dog along its sides rather than patting it on the head, which most dogs see as a threatening gesture. Don't encourage your dog to jump up and lick your face—you could get knocked over. To stop a dog from doing this, keep your hands by your sides and walk past it. Once it has stopped jumping, tell it to "Sit," then praise it. If it keeps jumping up, don't look at it and just leave the room.

Tooth brushing and nail clipping

Brushing can make your puppy's teeth last longer by preventing plaque from building up. It can also stop bad breath. Tooth brushing should be done by an adult, using special toothpaste and brushes available from pet stores. Most dogs' claws wear down as the dog walks, but if they grow too long, they need to be clipped. Let the vet clip the nails the first time, so that the adult in charge of the dog can learn how to do it without hurting the dog.

Training matters

Training a dog correctly is important. It teaches the dog to behave well with humans and other dogs. Untrained dogs can cause problems. They won't come when they're called, they pull on their leashes, and might try to attack other dogs or even bite humans.

One adult trainer

Although the whole family should make sure that a dog behaves correctly, one adult must be in charge of the training. If too many people are involved, your dog will get confused. Once your dog understands the basic commands taught by the adult, you can start to use them and join in the training, too.

Short and sweet

The best training involves a system of rewards and praise when the dog or puppy does as it is told. If it doesn't do as it's told, no reward is given until it does. Don't shout at your dog or punish it. Keep sessions to between five and fifteen minutes long because a dog can lose concentration easily. It's usually best to train your dog when it's hungry, because this makes it more eager for treats.

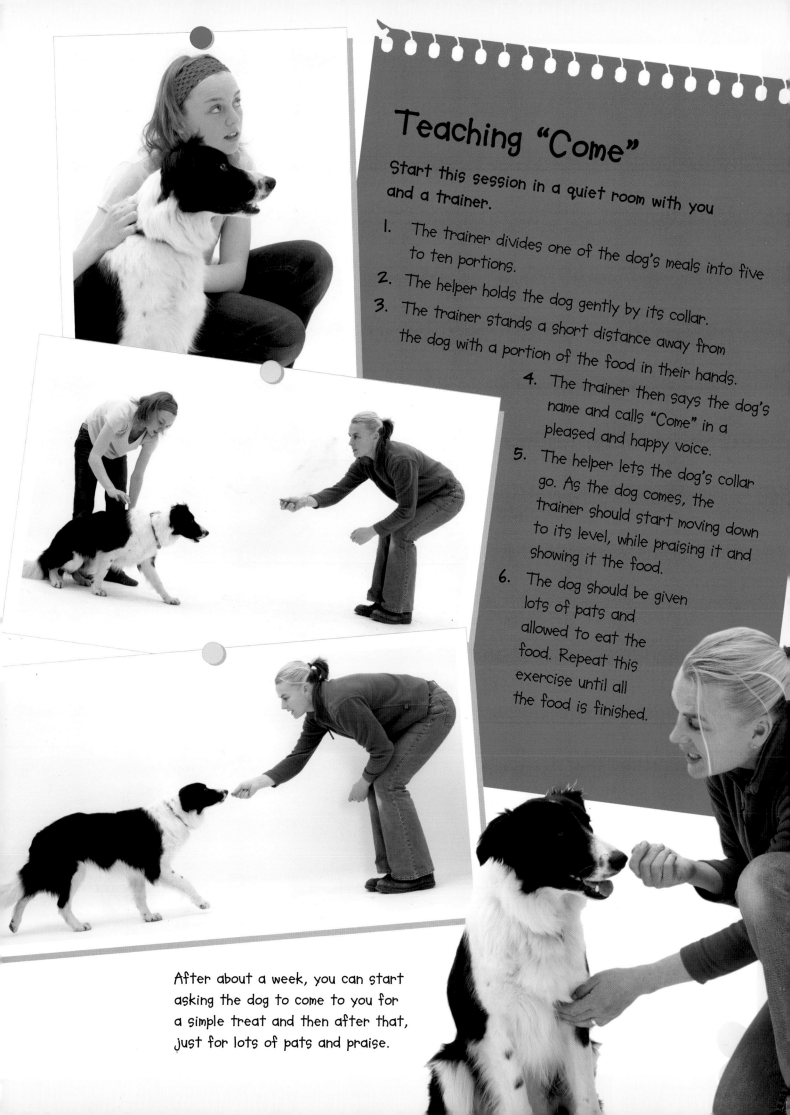

Teaching "Come"

Start this session in a quiet room with you and a trainer.

1. The trainer divides one of the dog's meals into five to ten portions.
2. The helper holds the dog gently by its collar.
3. The trainer stands a short distance away from the dog with a portion of the food in their hands.
4. The trainer then says the dog's name and calls "Come" in a pleased and happy voice.
5. The helper lets the dog's collar go. As the dog comes, the trainer should start moving down to its level, while praising it and showing it the food.
6. The dog should be given lots of pats and allowed to eat the food. Repeat this exercise until all the food is finished.

After about a week, you can start asking the dog to come to you for a simple treat and then after that, just for lots of pats and praise.

Outdoor training

When your puppy or dog is fully trained indoors, the next step is to teach it to come when you are outside. This can be harder because there will be more going on outdoors. You'll need an extendable leash and a toy or a dry dog-food treat to use as a reward.

Your dog's favorite toy can be used as a reward.

1. Call your puppy's name and say "Come."

2. If the puppy doesn't come, jerk the leash lightly to get its attention and try again. Don't use the lead to pull the puppy toward you.

3. When it comes, give the puppy lots of praise and a reward, such as a toy or a dog biscuit.

Training your dog to sit

Once your dog knows the command to come, you can try teaching "Sit."

1. Call your dog toward you using "Come" and show it the food treat.

2. When your dog is in front of you, move your hand containing the food over its head. It will try to keep its eyes on the food and will start to sit down.

3. As it does this, say "Sit" and give the treat. Once your dog has learnt the command, you can train it to respond when you say "Sit" from the side, front, or behind.

When your dog understands the commands, you won't have to give so many treats—the words and praise will be enough. When you give food treats, be careful how much you give. Training sessions should not make your dog fat!

Lead on

You must teach your puppy to walk on a leash. First, let your puppy get used to its leash. Clip the leash to the collar and leave your puppy to walk around the house for short periods of time.

Walking on a leash

The first step in teaching your dog to walk on a leash is teaching it to heel.

1. Start with the dog in the sit position—on your left side is best. Make sure its leash is kept quite short to keep the dog close to your body. Hold the other end of the leash in your right hand and a food treat in your left hand.

2. Start walking. Say your dog's name and "Heel," keeping your dog close to your left side. When it keeps by your side for a few paces, give it a small treat. Eventually your dog will make the connection and stop trying to pull away.

Furniture and food

Don't let your dog lie on furniture or beds because it will think that it's in charge, not you! Your dog could become very difficult to train and might start behaving badly. Don't feed your dog until after you are finished eating, and never feed it from the table. An adult should be in charge of feeding the dog.

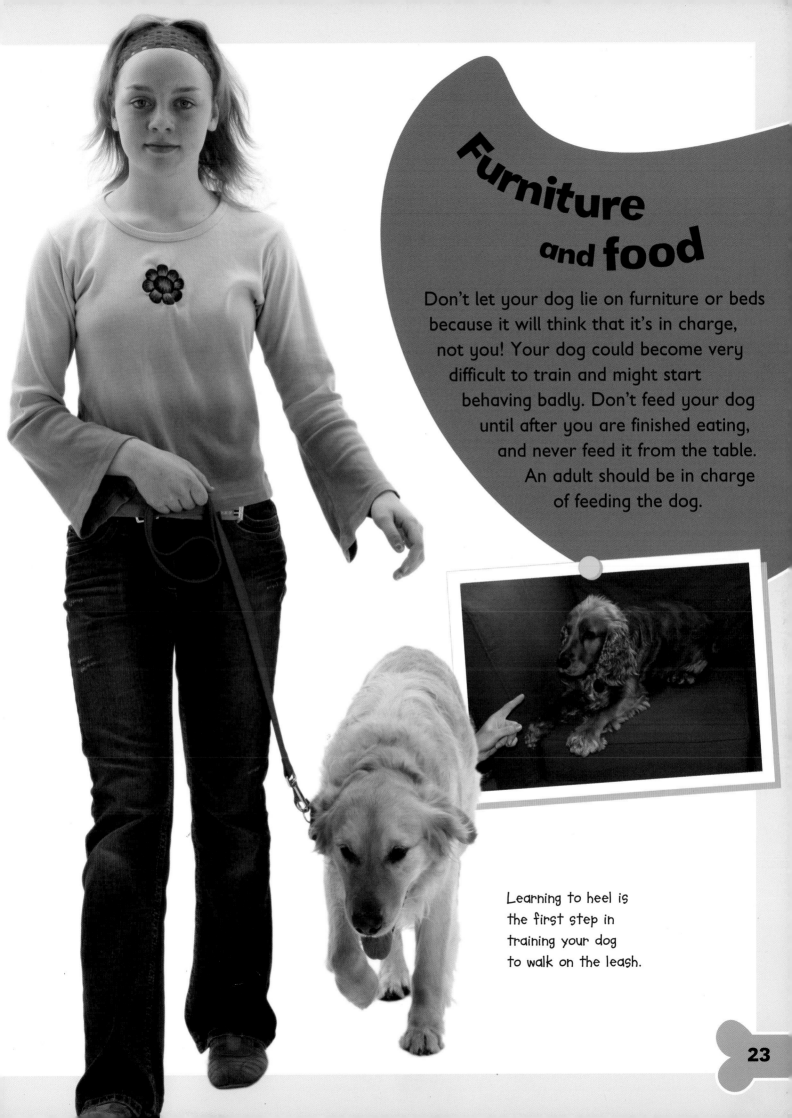

Learning to heel is the first step in training your dog to walk on the leash.

Playtime

Playing games is fun for both you and your dog. It's also great fun choosing toys for your pet because there are so many different types to choose from.

Choosing toys

Some toys are better than others, so make sure the ones you choose are good quality and safety tested. If your dog chews parts off the toy, throw the toy away and buy a new one. The pieces could get stuck inside your dog and require an operation to take them out. As time goes by, you'll get to know which toys your dog prefers!

Chewable toys

Don't give your dog old clothes or shoes to play with. It won't know the difference between clothes that are toys and those that aren't and will end up chewing your clothes, too. Large rubber chew toys that can be filled with healthy food treats are fun and they will stop your dog from chewing clothes or furniture. You can also buy chews and rubber, nylon, or sterilized bones from pet stores. Just about all dogs like bones to chew!

Sterilized bones are best because they have been specially prepared so that they don't contain any bacteria that could make your dog sick.

Other toys

Some dogs like twisted rope toys they can pull on. A ball is good for playing catch and fetch. Throw the ball away from the dog rather than toward it, in case the ball gets stuck in the dog's throat. Frisbees also make good toys. Never throw sticks for a dog, because it could be injured if it accidentally runs onto the end of the stick.

The adult in charge of training should give the toys out and pack them away after play. This will help to stop dogs becoming territorial and aggressive about their toys.

Hide and seek

Play a game of hide-and-seek with your pet. Tell the dog to "Stay." Show it a tasty treat or a toy and then let it see you hide it somewhere. Then say "Seek" and let it find the treat. Next time, tell the dog to "Stay," show it the treat, and pretend to hide it in several different places. Say "Seek" and make a big fuss of your dog when it finds it.

At the vet

A veterinarian will become one of your dog's best friends and an important source of dog care advice for the family. Look in the phone book or ask neighbors who have pets to recommend a vet in your area.

First visit

The first time your dog should see the vet is for a health check within the first two days of bringing it home. This is the time to ask for advice on spaying or neutering and vaccination against diseases such as rabies, **parvovirus** and **distemper**, which can kill dogs. Your vet will tell you how often your dog should be brought back for its **booster shots**.

Lost and found

Your vet can also microchip your dog and register your name and address on a database so that if your pet is ever lost, it can be returned to you. A microchip is as small as a grain of rice and is painlessly inserted under your dog's skin. Many animal shelters, vets, dog pounds, and police stations have scanners that can read the chip on any lost dog that is brought to them.

Fleas and worms

Your vet can treat your dog for worms and fleas. Regular worming is important because dog feces can contain Toxocara (roundworm) eggs, which can cause blindness in humans. Dogs can also suffer from other roundworms and tapeworms. If left untreated, worms can make your dog sick. Your puppy should be wormed every two weeks and an adult dog about every three to four months. If a dog is scratching a lot, it might have fleas. If so, ask the vet for a treatment to get rid of them.

To stop disease from spreading, the adult responsible for your dog should clean up after it, even if it has been wormed.

Fleas are brown parasites that run through a dog's fur and feed on its blood. They can cause rashes and infections in your dog's skin and can infest the whole house.

When is a dog unwell?

Take your dog to the vet if it seems sick. If it is uninterested in its food and its favorite games and toys, and is sleeping a lot more than usual, then it could be sick. Other signs of sickness include runny eyes and nose, diarrhea, vomiting, difficulty breathing, limping, and difficulty going to the bathroom.

Caring for an elderly dog

Just like elderly people, elderly dogs usually need special care to make sure they stay fit and healthy for as long as possible.

Tooth and claw

An older dog needs to be taken to the vet twice a year for checkups and to make sure its vaccinations are up to date. Your vet will check your dog's toenails because when dogs get older, they exercise less and their nails can overgrow and make their feet sore. The vet will check your dog's teeth— and possibly clean them, too—because dogs can get a buildup of **tartar** on their teeth, which can cause infections and loose teeth.

Extra comfort

As dogs get older, their joints may ache, so extra padding in a bed will provide comfort. If your dog gets very stiff, your vet may prescribe pills to make it more comfortable. Sometimes older dogs find it harder to see and hear. You can help them feel more at ease by not moving furniture around. Stick to regular times and routes for walks to make your pet feel more secure.

Bitch

Saying goodbye

If your pet is very sick, it might have to be
put to sleep. This is when the vet gives it
an injection so that it dies painlessly.
Afterwards, you can leave its body at the vet's
or have it buried in a pet cemetery. Your vet
might cremate your dog so that you can scatter
the ashes. It is very sad when a pet dies. You
may find it helpful to write a story, look at
pictures, or make a scrapbook
about your pet's life.

West Highland
white terrier

Labrador

How long do dogs live?

Small and medium-sized dogs, such as terriers
and spaniels, usually live to be about
15 years old. Larger dogs, such as
Afghan hounds, live for about 12 or
13 years, while very large dogs, such
as mastiffs, rarely live beyond
10 or 11 years old.

Afghan
hound

As it gets older,
your dog may like to
sleep more. Leave it
alone to rest and
it will come to you
when it is ready.

Glossary

booster shot   An extra shot of vaccine to keep a dog protected from disease

breed   A group of purebred dogs that share certain characteristics, such as coat color. Labradors and Airedales are examples of breeds

characteristics   Features such as color and length of coat, temperament and abilities

cower   When a frightened dog lowers its body to the ground

distemper   A deadly disease that causes high temperature, coughing and a runny nose and eyes

neuter   An operation that stops a dog being able to produce puppies

parvovirus   An infectious disease that dogs should be vaccinated against

tartar   A hard substance that can build up on a dog's teeth

temperament   The way that a dog behaves

Index

Notes for parents

Dogs and children

Owning a dog can be a wonderful experience for the whole family. However, it is also a big responsibility. Although this book has described certain dog care tasks that children can be involved in, the adults in the family are wholly responsible for the dog's wellbeing and the safety of children around it.

You should be certain that you can afford all necessary veterinary, training and kennel bills before getting a dog.

There should also be an adult at home most of the time, since it is unfair to leave a dog on its own for more than three hours a day.

Dog ownership can greatly benefit children because it can teach them about loyalty, responsibility, and care. However, there are safety rules that you need to keep in mind to make dog ownership as enjoyable as possible.

Safety checklist

- Dogs need to be walked twice a day. The adults in the family should take responsibility for this, because it can be dangerous for a child under the age of 16 to keep control of a dog.

- You must take responsibility for cleaning up your dog's waste when you take it out for walks. Dog feces can spread disease.

- To protect young children from being knocked down or bitten, they should not be left alone with a dog, and only adult members of the family should feed it.

- Do not allow a child to carry food near a dog, because the dog might try to snatch the food and knock the child over.

- Children should be taught to pet their dog—and any other dog—from the side and not from the front, and never to pat its head. Head patting is a dominant gesture that can make some dogs snap.

- Train your dog to lie down and stay when young children are playing together. If children are playing a game of ball and the dog tries to join in, the children could end up getting hurt.